For you whose heart is filled with the tragic and the comic at the same time.

About the HeART of HUMOR...

This book is written and designed for all those who believe that the gift of life is one of the rarest and most precious of all the gifts we've been blessed with.

It is written and designed for those who believe that the melodious sounds of laughter are in praise and appreciation of this wonderful gift of life.

Wrapped between simple explanations of the nuances and the benefits of laughter are seven simple language techniques which will highlight for you what makes us all laugh and how.

The accompanying ideas and thoughts will also help you differentiate the kinds of humor and choose the one that suits your sensitivities best.

The seven techniques will, after practice, make you

- A better observer of things
- An acute and sensitive listener
- A clearer and a faster thinker
- An entertaining host and speaker
- And, finally, an all-around happy and wholesome person to be with.

THE HEART OF HUMOR

TALES AND TECHNIQUES FOR A CREATIVELY FUNNIER YOU AT HOME AND AT WORK

RAJU MANDHYAN

Edited by:
Susan Evangelista &
Katrina Letargo

EMBASSY BOOKS
www.embassybooks.in

This edition first published in 2017

Published in India by:

Embassy Books
120, Great Western Building,
Maharashtra Chamber of Commerce Lane,
Fort, Mumbai - 400 023.
Tel : (91-22) 22819546 / 22818567.
Email : info@embassybooks.in
Website : www.embassybooks.in

Distribution Centres:

Mumbai, Ahmedabad, Bangalore, Kolkata, Chennai, Hyderabad, New Delhi, Pune

ISBN: 978-93-86450-10-4

In My opinion . . .

If we are all here to help others then what *exactly* are the others here for? The truth is that we are all here to help each other live a full life filled with love and laughter.

In my opinion our need for frequent indulgences in laughter comes second only to our need for love and loving. Just like the need for love, our need for laughter and, therefore, for psycho-physiological release builds up over time. Those that do not find occasion to feast or indulge in laughter are bound to fall victim to anxiety, depression and other ills.

I am sure most all of us have experienced moments with friends and family where laughter abounds and we come out deeply relieved and gladdened by these interactions. The reason is that laughter is a mental as well as an aerobic exercise nourishing us at the neuro-biological level. Laughter leaves us feeling light and filled with happiness.

For the memory of such moments and for the deep satisfaction they have provided us with, I invite you to participate in the understanding of what make us laugh, how we benefit from laughter and how to purposely create situations that generate laughter. This ability will become your wellspring to stimulating and satisfying all that is human and wonderful about life. I hereby, wholeheartedly, invite you to come, conceptualize, create and constantly indulge in humor at work, at home, or just about anywhere where laughter needs to be a part of the environment.

A person with a good sense of humor converts our lives into a never-ending adventure of ecstasy and fun. And, a person with a great sense of humor helps us achieve all our dreams except the ones where we see ourselves in the bare while at work.

Raju Mandhyan,
January 2016, Manila, Philippines

I Am Grateful...

...to all those who have ever made me laugh and recognize the essence of being alive.

...to all the teachers, trainers, speakers, coaches and friends who took the trouble of making me understand the value of authenticity and wit in communications.

...to the members of Toastmasters International, Asian Professional Speakers, Buzan Licensed Instructors around the world, National Speakers Association, Philippines Society for Training and Development and Team 69 of the Purposeful Stewardship Institute.

...to my friends Jess Liwanag, Toots de la Torre, Sylvia Mijares, Adrian Martinez, Padma Siap, Odessa Andal, Gina Mapua and all others who love being slightly loony.

...to those who bled and sweat with me, happily, while putting together this book namely; my editors Katrina Letargo and Susan Evangelista and my artists Alexander Sandoval and Clark Suano.

Thank you!
Raju Mandhyan

How to Make the Most out of this Book . . .

A sense of humor, many may argue, is something we are born with. I believe, though, that it can also be an acquired skill. In this book, squeezed between lightly handled theories and concepts are techniques that are easy to grasp and practice.

I recommend you read the book through then sit down with paper and pencil to master the techniques. You will have to, like most humorists and comedians, write and rewrite your material many times over. You will, equally, have to test and try your humor-material with friends and family until you achieve mastery over it and until humor becomes a habit to you. Should you, after all your efforts, continue to fail at becoming funny then please do remember to destroy all evidences.

Finally, keep the book handy and refer to it often when you write, socialize or conduct business. A word of caution and advice: Should this book somehow offend your sensitivities then make it your mission to form a support group, go out into the streets and rally to have this book banned and the author thrown behind bars.

In this latest edition, I am still of the same beliefs about humor and its impact on leadership communications and all I have done is added easy and benign examples which the leader-reader may emulate in her work.

Enjoy!

Raju Mandhyan,
January 2016, Manila, Philippines

Get FREE Insights

If you want to receive my sometimes deep and sometimes light articles on Communication Skills, Creativity and Leadership skills then please log on to www.mandhyan.com

Or send me an email at raju@mandhyan.com

Inside the Heart of Humor

Section 1

UNDERSTANDING

HUMOR

"There are three things which are real:
God, human folly, and laughter.
The first two are beyond
our comprehension.
So we must do
what we can with the third."
John F. Kennedy

Chapter 1

Humor and Laughter

In all the research I have done, which really is not much, and the books I have read, the trainings I have conducted, people inadvertently use the words humor and laughter synonymously.

"Humor", according to Stephen Leacock, the guru on the theory of humor, *"is the kindly contemplation of the incongruities of life and the artistic expression thereof."* In other words, humor is a feel- nice description of our flaws and follies. It is an artistic expression of the lop-sidedness of life and living. All other theories and explanations of humor are nothing but a rephrasing of this essential definition of humor. We laugh when the incongruities of life and living are highlighted and exaggerated. We also laugh when incongruities are created in our perceptions. Creating incongruities is also referred to as derailing the normal pattern of thought and all techniques on humor and comedy depend solely on this ability to derail thought, trip the mind, create surprise or let slip the tongue, etc.; This is the fulcrum which essentially mobilizes the fun and raises the levels of our happiness. Other than that our happiness levels can be raised and sustained in tandem with the amount of liquor we drink.

Consider a finely dressed man, briskly walking down the street, and being admired by onlookers. When, by chance, this man suddenly slips and falls, the crowd of onlookers can't help but burst out in laughter. The suddenness and the surprise snap the pattern of logical thinking and we couldn't but laugh out loud without restrain.

Now consider something as simple as this statement, *"I was wondering why the Frisbee was getting bigger, and then, it hit me!"*

Read that again slowly and see if it makes you smile or chuckle at the thought and the vision your mind creates. Here is what happens: Your mind was on track with the speaker wondering about the Frisbee, then the pun in the world "hit" tripped your thoughts as did the vision of someone being hit by it and you chuckled.

This trip, this incongruity, generates amusement and fun because our brain is programmed to follow logic, structure and sequence. When the sequence is broken or the structure tripped, it generates a result in the brain which is like a mental knee jerk. This mental knee jerk sends a signal to the abdomen which in response releases air into and through our lungs, larynx and the vocal chords releasing chuckles, laughter or guffaws.

During laughter our stomach muscle exerts effort. Our arms, legs and shoulder muscle tense up. Our facial muscles squeeze upwards and our blood pressure spikes up. In effect, we get one hale and hearty workout. Laughter tones our bodies, shapes our muscles and puts a glow on our faces. So, do not be surprised if after finishing this book and mastering the skills of humor, you tone up, acquire a chiseled chest, a wash-board tummy and end up looking like a movie-star!

Laugher, thus, is the outcome of humor. Laughter is the physical manifestation of humor while humor is the sense and the skill to create laughter. Learning to laugh is learning to develop a sense of humor and mastering the skills of humor by observing, contemplating and artistically expressing the flaws, the follies and the lopsidedness of life. Yes, life.

Your life and living will always be source-eternal and the material for creating humor and humor is the machinery that will fill all that is somber, sad and solemn around you with sounds of laughter. Laughter, which is one of the main reasons that life still remains popular even though the cost of living goes up daily.

The Lighter Side of Darkness

As I closed my eyes and stepped into his shoes, a chilling feeling engulfed my very soul.

The feeling of a loathsome loneliness.
The feeling of a gut-chewing, ferocious fear.
And, the feeling of a death-like darkness.

And yet, somehow, from within me, I found the courage to laugh just like he had done, like this: Ha! Ha! Ha!

I know! I know! I've gone ahead and you want to know who "he" is, and what am I talking about? I will tell you! But first let me tell you how I met him.

All of last year, I was depressed over several things:
I was depressed because business was bad.

I was depressed because my money wasn't going far.
I was depressed because I was gaining weight and losing hair.
In fact, I was depressed about being depressed over such silly things.

One day, during this depression, I was driving home from another failed sales call. The world around me was a sad place to be in when I stopped for a traffic light on the corner of Shaw and Edsa. Pedestrians were scurrying home, cars were snarling at each other, and thirty feet above me the Light Rail Transit was hurtling away towards nowhere.

I felt sorry for the world, and I didn't feel any good about myself either.

Then, suddenly, right in the path of my car appeared a man.
His clothes were tattered, his hair was long, and his silhouette was messiah-like. "Uh-oh!" I said to me, "Another one of those Looney tunes!"

As he groped towards my car with an open palm, I rolled down the window hoping to get rid of him with a few coins. Ladies and Gentlemen, on that sad, dusky evening, the face that I looked into made me jump out of my skin. Dust-covered, laden with scars, it was a face from another world. Where his eyes should have been, there were two holes of darkness!

I gently dropped the coins into his palm, for a moment he seemed to stare at me. He then thanked me and laughed heartily. Ha! Ha! Ha!

Laughed heartily? How could he? Was he not blind? Was he not a beggar on the streets? Where'd he get the gumption to laugh, let alone exist in this depressing world?

That is when my wandering soul abandoned me and stepped into his shoes. In his shoes I felt his loneliness, his fear, and darkness. In his shoes, I realized that the blind man was laughing in spite of his blindness.
I drove away from the corner thinking:
So what if my business was bad; at least I wasn't bankrupt!
So what if my money wasn't going far; at least I wasn't broke!
So what if I was gaining weight and losing hair; I still had a great smile!

Oftentimes, we take our shortcomings and setbacks much too seriously. We dwell so much on the negative that we forget to see the humor behind things.

How many times have we lost opportunities because we thought we were not tall enough, not rich enough or not skilled enough?
How many times have we broken relationships because we thought we didn't get enough freedom, appreciation, or understanding?

Had we looked on the brighter side, we could have survived!

Had we looked on the lighter side, we could have shone!

Like:
Danny de Vito who is short, bald, and ugly, and yet he is a successful actor, director, and producer.
Former Filipino Senator Juan Flavier is short, bald, comes from a humble background but he still went ahead and became the most famous Senator ever!
Comedian Marissa Sanchez constantly pokes fun at herself and becomes more and more successful.

They all started by looking at the bright side and making light of their shortcomings. Not only did they surpass their shortcomings; they outshone others.
So: If our businesses are not making profits, think of the lighter side – turn them into non-profit organizations!

If our money is not going far, think of the lighter side – at least it's getting there faster!
If we are turning old and ugly on the outside, at least on the inside we are becoming wiser and more beautiful!

The change in our external behavior will change the way we think. The way we think and act will change our lives and our destinies!

Laugh at your failures and laugh at your foibles! Laugh if you are fat and laugh if you are thin!

Laugh and your loneliness, your fears and your dejections will fizzle away!

I maintain that we may have come into this world helpless and crying; but it is within our power and capacity to go out laughing.

Laugh! Laugh! Laugh!

Taken from "the HeART of Public Speaking"
by Raju Mandhyan

"To truly laugh, you must be able to take your pain and play with it!"
Charlie Chaplin

Chapter 2
Depth and Meaning

I was in my early teens when I read the poetry of Mirza Abdullah Ghalib, the 19th Century romantic poet of India. From the scores of verses Mirza Ghalib had written, one left an indelible imprint on my mind. It went thus:

"Dard jab had se guzar jaata hai,
Tab dawa ban jaata hai"

"Pain, when it crosses a certain threshold,
Turns into medicine and heals rather than hurts."

To my young, inquisitive mind, the idea seemed a bit strange and unbelievable. How could pain, sorrow or tragedy heal and ultimately become the cure? If that was the case, why were all the people in the world shying away from pain and suffering at all? Shouldn't they be seeking, appreciating and wooing pain?

It wasn't till years later when I read Kahlil Gibran's "The Prophet" did I come to realize the sublime depth of Mirza Ghalib's emotions. In "The Prophet", Kahlil Gibran concedes- *"pain is the breaking of the shell of understanding."* Surely and truly, when it exceeds and crosses a certain threshold, our pain slowly evolves and leads us into a deeper understanding of ourselves, our frailties and most of all, our humanity.

Pain and suffering induces profound introspection and introspection eventually gifts us with humanity, compassion and wisdom. All of us often get entangled with the daily trappings of life and fate. During such times our minds struggle for a way out, a way out into peace and relief. During such times, our minds and emotions work overtime, and by introspection, delve into the deepest abyss of our psyches.

Eventually, after a period of torment and anguish, relief does come. When relief comes, we look back at the pettiness of our entrapments, the inanity of our struggles and we laugh! We laugh at the recognition of our frailty and we laugh at life. This innate ability to discern and accept our fragile nature is the seed of humor. This is also referred to as ***anagnorisis_****tragic recognition or insight.*

I especially remember one summer during my teens when I learned to look beyond my own pettiness and I learned to laugh through my tears and pain. We used to then live in a quiet neighborhood in Pune, India. One afternoon I was sitting by the window of our fourth floor apartment and watching some of friends play by a tree on the street below. The day was, as is usual in India, hot and uncomfortable but from the sounds of their laughter, the boys seemed to be enjoying every minute of it. They would climb up, try to catch each other, and jump down with a whoop. I felt left out and lonely at my perch by the window. Mom had grounded me for the day as she had done so many times in the last few months.

She'd been hard and mean with most everyone in the family ever since she'd come from the hospital a few months ago. Prior to her treatments, she used to be a busybody around the house and everything was well between us. Lately, she'd manage the household chores through her shrill commands and scolding at all those around her. I didn't quite understand the change in her behavior and all I wanted was the freedom to go and play with my friends in the street below. A child like me, I thought, ought to t be having fun and laughing like kids should.

I was lost in my reverie when Didee, my elder sister, quietly sneaked up on me. "What are you thinking?" she asked. As I turned and looked at her tall and slender figure, I realized that Mom had been much harder on her than others. She looked pale and tired from having to attend to Mom's constant needs and commands. "Uh, nothing, I was just about to get up and iron my clothes for school tomorrow," I replied. "Would you like me to iron them for you?" she offered. "Nope, you'll probably get another tongue-lashing from Momma," I replied.

I set up the ironing board besides the window and plugged in the iron. I'd just begun to iron one of the only two shirts I had for school when the shrieks of joy from the street, drew me back to the window. The boys were all over the tree climbing swinging and laughing and I so wanted to part of all that excitement. I stayed glued to the window for a while when suddenly I felt someone pull me by my ear, "You've burned your shirt, you idiot!" she yelled. I looked down, the iron had scorched its way through my shirt collar and my world came crashing down at me. Mom let loose hell upon me that summer afternoon.

Later, at night, as I lay in bed with a sore ear and a bruised ego, I decided to do what I'd been planning to do for weeks. Come morning, I'd run away from home and from Mom. I'd had enough of living like this. I wanted freedom and I wanted peace. Next morning, while it was still dark, I packed a back pack and threw in a picture of me and Mom we'd taken at a carnival a year ago. As I pulled on my sandals, I knew had no idea where I'd be going to but I had a good idea what I was getting away from. I was getting away from torture and pain. Slowly, I sneaked out of the house into a night that was beginning to turn into day.

I'd barely covered a few blocks when, in the distance, I saw a shadow of a boy running towards me. The street was empty and the figure running toward me was awkward and out of skew. His arms were flailing and he seemed to limping on one leg. He was moving fast and clumsily towards me. As he got closer, I heard sobbing loudly and his face was covered with tears and dirt. He looked very sad and unhappy. As he passed by me, I realized his clumsy gait was the cause of a club foot and polio-ridden limbs. He was about my age but he looked very sunburned, scrawny and sad.

After he'd passed me by, I stood my ground and wondered what could be making him so sad, so afraid. Were his troubles bigger than mine? What, in my own life, could be worse than his? I looked down at my legs, my arms and the way I was dressed. I looked good to me! I thought about the things that were burdening my heart and I realized that they definitely could not match the things that he'd probably suffered in his life.

I sat down on the pavement and pulled out Mom's picture from the bag. She looked wholesome, strong and giving. I looked content and happy by her side. Things then were good for us and for me. Gently a tear rolled down my cheek and fell on the picture as I remembered the conversation she'd had with her Doctor several months ago, "Mrs. Mandhyan," he'd said "the treatments will be long and exhausting. You will lose weight, get stomach cramps and may also become irritable."

As I remembered the past, I began to understand the present. The pain inside of me began to melt away and a warm, deep understanding towards my Mom began to take over. My shoulders relaxed, I took a deep breath and smiled. I stayed there, on the pavement for a while as the sun rose and soaked me in its warm and happy glow.

As the streets of Pune began to get filled with people going to their work, I stood up and walked back home. As I approached our street corner, I saw two feminine silhouettes waiting by the entrance to our apartment building. At first glance, I knew that would be Mom and Didee. I ran fast and straight into the open arms of my Mom. There were tears in her eyes but her smile told me that she too had begun to understand tings unseen by her. For a long while, she held me against her heart. I was silently laughing inside.

Ages have passed since that day but I still remember and I still feel happy with the memory of that moment and of that understanding.

Humor and pain like comedy and tragedy have subtle similarities. At the root level, these are both essentially the same. A person who has suffered great pain and tragedy in life also has the ability to transcend from it and convert it to comedy.

If you look through the history of those who have made the world laugh, you will note that they did, indeed, suffer great sorrow and pain before discovering laughter.

The bard, Shakespeare, created immortal masterpieces of drama but lived a personal life wrought in longing and loneliness. His every work is a constant dance between the tragic and the comic.

Charlie Chaplin, the lovable champ, grew up in a world surrounded by poverty and Dickensian angst; almost all of his movies depict scenes of glee and sadness sublimely mixed and exaggerated for theatrical effect.

The legendary Doctor Patch Adams, who proved to the world that, indeed, laughter is the best medicine, lived a life of hardship and struggle, until and even after he acquired a medical degree. His patients loved his clowning and humor because they knew that behind the facade, he deeply understood, felt and also shared their pain. His humorous nature to them was healing because they knew and understood its source and they could relate to it from their own depths.

Kahlil Gibran also wrote:

"The self – same from which your laughter rises was oftentimes filled with your tears."

Very often when we are laughing uncontrollably, we find tears streaming down our faces. And, quite as often, after we've exploded our pain through crying, we find ourselves laughing joyfully. Both laughing and crying provide cathartic cleansing. Our facial expressions, too, mirror this kinship. That's why, at times, it is hard to make out if one is crying or laughing! Somewhere in the depths of our soul; somewhere in the recesses of our limbic brain, laughing and crying are separated by a very thin wall just as comedy and tragedy are.

A recognition of this semblance between crying and laughing, and of tragedy and comedy, will further our edge to grasping humor. We will develop an ability to see beyond what is, and discover meaning and serendipity in living. This understanding will also make it easy for us to consciously source, convert, repack and deliver humor on call. This ability to sight, search, reassemble and generate humor will also give us conscious control and help us transcend pain and suffering with elegance.

Socrates once commented on the medical theory of his day:

"As it is not proper to heal the eyes without the head,
Nor the head without the body;
So neither is it proper to cure the body without the spirit"

The word "heal" comes from the root word "haelen" which means to "make whole". In modern dictionaries, it is also defined as a state of mind, mood and spirit. It is also defined as an ability of being laughable and comical. Humor, therefore, is also wholeness and balance through laughter. Laughter, as a whole body exercise, binds the body, mind and spirit to bring about – healing.

[NOTE: I sneaked this in so you could use it in defense of buying this book. Or, you could use it to impress members of the opposite sex at a cocktail party. *"Yes," you could say, "after great deliberation on the nuances of humor, I agree absolutely with Socrates that it is all about wholeness, balance and coming together."]*

Chunk It Down

Society lady playing dominoes with friends gets a call from her housemaid, "Ma'am, your cat fell off the roof and died!"

Society Lady screams and collapses on the floor, unconscious.

Back home from the Emergency Room, she admonishes the house help and instructs her to chunk down all bad news in the future.
"Next time when something like this happens, you must first call and say,
Ma'am the cat is on the roof then an hour later you must call and say,
Ma'am the cat fell off the roof.
Finally, another hour later, you must say, Ma'am the cat is dead. That way I won't be so traumatized. Ok?"

"I get it, I get it!" replies the housemaid, excitedly.

Weeks later, Society Lady is again playing dominoes with her friends when she gets a call from her housemaid,

"Ma'am, here's the first part, ***your husband is on the roof."***

Mighty Nice

"You haven't taken proper care of your good wife," the divorce court judge ruled. "I am going to allot her $2,000 a month."

"Oh, that's mighty nice of you, Your Honor, I will, also from time to time, give her a few dollars myself."

"Comedy has had no history, because it was not, at first, treated seriously."
Aristotle

Chapter 3
History and Origins

There are several other schools of thought pertaining to laughter and humor. I personally subscribe to the theory that we laugh because our bodies are hard-wired for it. We laugh because every single cell of our body wants to!

Another school of thought dates back to our ancient predecessors–the cavemen. Whenever faced with danger, their shrieks of terror, from sheer helplessness, turned into hysterical laughter. This belief is comparable to that of humor being the thin wall dividing pain, pleasure, and healing. Whenever faced with extreme danger, out of helplessness, we reach over and out into its ludicrous side and we laugh.

A third school of thought on humor states that we laugh because laughter served as a means of happy communication before any form of language was developed by humans. Laughter was part and parcel of grunts, growls, barks, roars, hisses, shrieks and screams. Smiles, chuckles and laughter were the signs of relief and happiness. Laughter, as it still does, during the pre-historic age also served as recognition of companionship and camaraderie.

Several other theories on laughter and its evolution similarly claim that we laugh because we feel good when we compare ourselves to others who were, and are too short, too fat, too tall or too ugly. We ridicule and laugh at the expense of others because we see incongruence and we feel secure knowing that it isn't happening to us.

Again, things haven't changed much since we've moved up from the caves to skyscrapers. We claim to have evolved from the apes and yet there are thousands of apes amongst us.

One of the most interesting take on humor comes from the history of medicine: It relates to the etymology of the word "humor" which originates from the Latin "humor" meaning wet or moist. Hippocrates, the father of modern medicine, introduced the theory of four bodily fluids based on the four elements of nature – earth, wind, fire and water. The *choleric* person, according to Hippocrates, has too much yellow bile or fire in him. He is angry, upset and rages all the time. He is the guy who never goes to bed angry, he stays up nights and plots his revenge on the world. The *melancholic* has too much black bile or earth in him. He can be quiet, miserable and forlorn at the same time. He is the person who is constantly lost in unfamiliar territory—his own mind. The *sanguine* has too much blood or air in him. He moves fast, is cheerful and upbeat like a chimpanzee on cocaine. Lastly, the *phlegmatic* has too much water in him. He can be placid, matter-of-fact and unconcerned. He's a person who gets angry without any enthusiasm.

Just like the relationship between tragedy and comedy, it is the melancholic person who can be comedic and tragic. As cited before, people like Mirza Ghalib, Shakespeare and Charlie Chaplin fall in the melancholic category. The depths and the brilliance of their work on humor and literature stems from the fact that they could introspect, brood and have sudden flashes of comedic brilliance about their plots and characters. Yes, Mirza Ghalib also has several works of rhyme and rhythm that have dark, satirical twists to them.

Put all these historical inferences together and give them their due, *kindly contemplation* and you will notice that Stephen Leacock's definition of humor supersedes all.

And, we want to laugh because our physio-psychological nature needs it just as we, many a times, feel the urge to park diagonally in a universe parked parallel.

Ouch!

Back in the medieval times, there was an archery contest.

They stood a boy by the tree with an apple on his head for target. Along comes the first archer, in blue tights. He deftly picks up the bow and arrow, takes aim and shoots. "Zip!" He hits the apple right in the center, turns to the crowd and claims, "I am William Tell!"

Along comes another archer, in green tights, confidently picks up the bow and arrow, takes aim, lets go. "Zap!" He hits the tail-end of the first arrow, splits it into two and pierces the apple right in the center, turns to the crowd and declares, "I am Robin Hood!"

*Along comes the third archer, **Raju Mandhyan**, in pink tights. He **daintily** picks up the bow and arrow, gently takes aim and lets go. "Zooops!" He hits the boy in the eye, turns to the crowd and says, "I **am** sorreee!"*

"I see humor as food. An adequate share of humor and laughter represents an essential part of the diet of the healthy person."

Norman Cousins

Chapter 4
Kinds and Differences

Just as humor and laughter are used synonymously, we also confuse jokes as humor and humor, sometimes, as comedy. They are interrelated, but each has its own distinguishing characteristics.

Jokes are funny but jokes alone do not make up humor. Jokes are ready-made and are not usually spontaneous. Sometimes they are situational and relevant but humor is and should always be. Like humor, jokes are dependent on the same principle of incongruity between two things or more. Jokes also depend upon derailment of thinking patterns and are, by themselves, elements for creating humor.

Comedy, on the other hand, is a combination of several kinds of humor. It can be harsh, intense and, at times, mean. Humor should be pleasing, lighter, relevant and a part of everyday interactions. Humor, too, should be instrumental in the improvement and nurturing of individuals and communities, Amen.

Hence, humor may be jokes, gags, slapstick but humor, more than all these, is about balance, wholesomeness and the acceptance of our frailty. In this context, humor is an essential element of creativity and humility. It goes beyond just recognizing life as it is, but it is the ability to enthusiastically say to life – *"Yes"!*

The variations of humor come from the way it is packaged and presented, including the objects and behavior it ridicules. Most all kinds of humor is packaged and presented in three different forms: Physical, Visual and Verbal.

Physical Humor involves bodily motions. Under this form of humor we laugh at bumps, slips, falls, tumbles and silly antics by clowns and mimics. In this kind of created humor, the actor seemingly suffers a series of mishaps blunder but quickly recovers, pretends nothing happened, and goes on with life. *Yes, life!*

Charlie Chaplin, Buster Keaton, Red Buttons, The Three Stooges, Laurel and Hardy all used a lot of physical humor. The creation of physical humor, again, is also dependent on the theory of pain and derailment. Observers of this kind of humor sense the pain the actors might be going through then laugh at being relieved that – hey, nothing really happened! Prior to the bump or slip of the actor, the mind of the observer was expecting things to proceed normally. But when the blunder does occur, mental derailment takes place and we laugh.

Visual Humor is a little more stationary than physical humor. Here laughter is created by visual comparisons. For example, Laurel and Hardy standing side by side, fat against thin, dressed as they do become cause for laughter.
Arnold Schwarzenegger and Danny de Vito, again, standing side by side with Arnold in shorts and Danny in a suit, for the movie titled “Twins”, become cause for amusement too. Oh, ok, just for a chuckle.

Rowan Atkinson’s humor, as Mr. Bean, has a lot of visual humor rather than the physical one. Mr. Bean does not fall, slip or get hit on the head but he is extremely expressive, makes really weird faces and silly body movements. How lethal visual humor can be is proved by the fact how middle-aged folks stay away from tight clothes and flimsy lingerie.

The third classification, you have probably guessed it by now – my favorite – is **Verbal Humor.** Words and sentences so put together to stir up imagination, churn up emotions, expose the unseen and make us laugh. Words and sentences so put together so as to glorify or insult our very intelligence. Yummy!

Verbal humor is what this book is all about. It is about re-arranging or adjusting the blocks in our minds through play of words, choice of adjectives, figures of speech, form, structure, good timing and vocal variety.

From these three main modes of expressing humor, the following varieties are created using different references and context.

Burlesque is mostly comedy taken to a sarcastic extreme. Characters overdress, overact and sarcastically highlight the unusual about people and their interactions. Comedy theatre is spiced up with this kind of humor. The old – time skits between George Burns and his wife, the skits on shows like "Saturday Night Live" all have the Burlesque flavor. Burlesque can be uncouth and loaded with innuendo.

Anecdotal Humor is usually very tame and is a reflection on the little ups and downs of our daily lives. In Anecdotal humor though there may be exaggeration, understating and cause for derailment of mind they just are not as severe as they are in other forms of humor. Anecdotal humor seldom lets audiences roll into the aisles laughing, but it can leave them amused and happy.

Here's an example:

Sometime in the late 80's I was flying from London to Mumbai and I got to sit next to a Gandhi look-alike. He had an aisle seat by the kitchen which had a better view of the movie monitor hung from the plane's ceiling. At night, when the lights were turned off, Rocky III was being shown. I requested Gandhi to switch seats, since he wasn't watching the movie and he kindly obliged.

Halfway through the movie, in the darkness, the stewardess came by and plopped a food tray in front of me as she did with a few others. With my eyes glued to Rocky III and my ears covered, I opened the food box and began to eat some kind of bland vegetables and rice. Through the side of my eyes, I saw Gandhi staring at my food and sometimes at me. What a rude man, I thought to myself, why can't he wait till his food arrives? The food in my mouth was tasteless and boring but, hey, Rocky and I were busy beating up Mr. T to a pulp.

Later, as the movie ended and the lights were turned on, several stewardesses began to lay food trays in front of everyone else except the few who'd already eaten. This included me. When the food boxes were being opened up a pungent aroma of mutton curry drifted to my nostrils. Gandhi, next to me, let out a stifled scream when he opened his box. Obviously, he hated red meat not knowing that is not red meat that is bad fuzzy green meat that is bad for people.

Slowly, as I realized what had happened, I turned to meet his accusing eyes. Boy was I glad he was a strict vegetarian! Otherwise, he'd have eaten me alive for cheating him out of his specially ordered food.

After apologizing profusely, I was able to make up by getting him several bowls of fruit and salad from the pantry. Unfortunately, my strict vegetarian friend, stayed unhappy and distant for the rest of the flight.

Parodies are musicals and musical comedies which make fun of relationship flaws, lost-loves, and the flip side of trends and cultures. Parodies are a combination of physical, visual and verbal humor. Shakespeare's "Comedy of Errors" or "Twelfth Night or What You Will" plus the plays of Neil Simon are all forms of parodies.

Satires make fun of celebrities, movie stars, icons and all those in positions of power. A satire is a literary work holding up human vices and follies to ridicule or scorn. It can be very stinging and painful. Satires were often used in days of little or no press freedom for purposes of political change. George Orwell's classic book, "Animal Farm", ridiculed social systems in a mild but extremely effective way. The caricatures of R.K. Laxman of India and Larry Alcala of the Philippines have been poking fun at all political and social powers-that-be for decades.

Dark Humor, like dark chocolate, is one of my favorite forms. It deals with taboo subjects like death, disease, the dark side of human nature and social systems. These are subjects and issues that people, in general, fear discussing in the open, even though they are stark proofs of our own frailties. The poem "Death" by Robert Brown, the works of Woody Allen depict dark humor. The movie," War of the Roses", starring Michael Douglas and Katherine Turner dangerously expose the after effects of a marriage that is dying in spirit. Former lovers, Michael and Katherine, attack, maraud and finally kill each other in the movie. Its plot comes very dangerously close to the reality and hate that builds up in broken relationships and yet is a viciously funny spectacle. With dark humor, tackling such issues is like taking a bull by its horns, claiming our stake on life and declaring our lust for living.

Studying these varieties and discerning the mechanism that goes behind creating humor will enhance your skills and will also deepen and develop your understanding of human nature. Your mastery will come when you travel these paths for you to resolve and repackage the follies of life and thus deliver them for the benefits of others, with grace, sensitivity and style.

With this, we more or less, wrap up the significance, history, etymology and variations of humor. For the next few pages while overwhelming you with its multi-faceted benefits, this book will start leading you into creating and delivering humor with impact. The book will quicken your wit and reflexes which sometimes can be a great substitute for poor table manners. The new techniques you learn will have audiences listen to you more closely for all your slips and falls.

Smashing!

Kishu and Nanu are out drinking when Kishu, after a few too many, keels over.
Nanu calls 911 and screams, "I think my friend just died from too much liquor. What do I do?"

A quiet, controlled voice at the other end says, "First take a deep breath, get a hold on yourself and then make sure he's really dead."

After a pause, the operator hears a bottle smash against a head followed by an eerie moan. Nanu gets back to the phone. "That's done," he whispers to the operator. "What do I do next?"

Peacefully!

"When I die, I want to go peacefully like my Grandfather did, in his sleep -- not screaming, like the passengers in his car!"

Section 2

BENEFITS OF HUMOR

"When humor goes, there goes civilization."
Erma Bombeck

Chapter 5

Physiological and Psychological

Besides being one of the best ice-breakers and a top of the line aphrodisiac, the benefits of humor far exceed the benefits of basic exercises because the aerobic effects generated by laughter, as explained in Chapter 1, originate from the brain, hence, it is the mind that gets the workout first and the visible signs of that workout, later, are seen on the body.

When we laugh more than twenty muscles squeeze and push the blood around in our faces and makes us glow with happiness. Vigorous laughter activates our tear ducts and studies have shown that tears, whether happy or sad, always reduce stress. Scientists have also found that after laughing, the saliva in our mouth develops higher levels of disease-fighting immunologlobins and killer T- cells, thereby enhancing our levels of resistance.

Within our chest, the quick and voluminous exhaling and inhaling during laughter also strengthens our lungs. A healthy respiratory system is key to pumping and exchanging more oxygen within our blood. Stronger inner linings of our blood vessels, also known as endothelium, release good chemicals like nitric oxide thereby reducing clotting and inflammation in our blood vessels.

Laughter, which induces increased oxygen levels to the blood, not only strengthens the vessels of our heart but also is beneficial to the upkeep and nourishment of our brain. An increased and a better quality of blood inflow to our brain make it resilient, quick and creative in response. The medicinal benefits of laughter were known even during biblical times, thus the proverb*, "a merry heart doeth good like medicine".*

American Indian, Ojibwa tribes were also known to have performed mimicking and clowning as part of their processes to heal several kinds of illnesses.

Recently, the one who really brought the medicinal and physiological benefits of laughter to the fore was Norman Cousins, a former writer and subsequently a professor at UCLA. Prior to his becoming a professor, he was affected by a serious collagen disease that affects the connective tissues. Recognizing the medicinal benefits of laughter and the relationship between stress and sickness, he figured that if he would reverse the process of stress he might gain an edge over his sickness. He, consequently, used laughter through a daily diet of comedy combined with large and strong intakes of Vitamin C.

After winning his battle with his sickness, Cousins reported, *"ten minutes of laughter would provide me with at least two hours of pain-free sleep".* The process of stress had been reversed and Norman Cousins went down in history as the man who truly turned laughter into medicine. Today, because of Cousin's work and success, we concur to laughter's analgesic effect on our bodies as an everyday occurrence.

Today, we accept and approve the many physiological benefits of laughter. We also concur with the old saying, *"a healthy mind creates a healthy body and a healthy body does house a healthy mind*." We have come to accept that our bodies are not separate from our minds and neither is our mind separate from our bodies. They are, in fact, one single entity and one single bundle of energy.

Currently in India, and in many parts of the world, my friends, Dr. Madan Kataria and, his wife Madhuri, of Mumbai have introduced and started social clubs that get together and for hours "laugh without reason."

In the early 90's, Madan, a physician by profession, used to go for a stroll in the neighborhood where he and his friends, at the end of their walks, would share jokes and laughter. Over time they realized they were enjoying the laughter more than the walk and the same, silly jokes. That realization sparked off his research into the benefits of laughter and led him into the Upanishads, a set of texts that form the basis of all Yoga. Dr. Kataria rediscovered the relationship of laughter and Yoga, long known to ancient India. Today, across the world, Laughter Clubs are a rage and scores of people in Europe, USA and many parts of Asia get together and indulge in life-nurturing "laughter without reason". Their minds and bodies, however, are secretly and continuously benefiting from this happy exercise form.

Should you or your team want to experience how laughter perks up your body and creates an adrenalin rush, let me share with you a seven-step exercise I, usually, conduct in my creativity and humor workshops.

Step One: Have your team stand tall, erect and yet ease with feet spread apart slightly. Slowly but deliberately inhale and exhale deeply for one whole minute.

Step Two: Take your first two-fingers, place them on your forehead, tilt up your elbow like a boy scout and then laugh out loud and quick from the depths of your belly. Let out the sounds of Hi Hi Hi for five to seven times.

Step Three: Now place your fingers on your throat, elbow up and then laugh out loud and quick from the depths of your belly. Let out the sounds of He He He for five to seven times.

Step Four: Quickly move your fingers onto the center of your chest, press lightly, and then laugh out loud and quick from the depths of your belly. Let out the sounds of Ha Ha Ha for five to seven times.

Step Five: Place your fingers at a spot few inches above your belly button, press lightly, and then like Santa Claus, laugh out loud and quick from the depths of your belly. Let out the sounds of Ho Ho Ho five to seven times and make them loud enough to wake up all the kids in the neighborhood.

Step Six: Move your fingers down to few inches below your belly button, not too low, press lightly and, for five to seven times, laugh out loud with the sounds of Hu Hu Hu. Should you feel an urge to go after this step, I beg you to hold on for a while longer for the finale.

Step Seven: From the top, start over with your forehead and the sounds of Hi Hi Hi and medley all the way down to Hu Hu Hu at lightning speed, gusto and all the energy you can gather.

Repeat the seventh step until your laughter becomes rhythmic and spontaneous. Do this until you feel well worked out and stop before someone sends you all off to the crazy house.

At the end of this exercise you will feel elated and as if you've run around the largest block in your life. This exercise is called the **IEAOU** laughter and may only be repeated commercially after seeking an explicit written permission by the author.

To continue:

The outward expression of the mental knee-jerk, as we have learned, is an explosion of air and mirth from the pits of our bellies. This aerobic exercise, which pumps up an increased and better quality of oxygenated blood into our brains, enhances the responsiveness of our mental faculties. The mind, thereby, works the body and the body, in return, nourishes the mind. This cyclical relationship works better and faster through laughter created a good mastery of humor skills.

At another level, humor also creates balanced thinking. A set-up in a joke, based on the theory of incongruity, follows a logical pathway which is essentially a left-brain activity. The logic is then compared with existing emotional memories and visual records in the right brain. The punch-line, usually at the end, triggers a logical-creative reaction in the mind causing the physical explosion and outburst called laughter.

Contrarily, a visual verbal incongruence sets up the right brain by showing what is, but referring to it as something else. For instance – a huge guy when called "Tiny" creates laugher. In essence, humor lets the right brain and the left brain play "see-saw" thereby strengthening the whole brain. All such humorous exertions and exercise help broaden our thinking and heighten our creativity.

The science bchind memorizing well, Mnemonics, also employs the same principle in increasing our memory retention. For memory enhancement exercises, people are asked to take a bunch of names, numbers or images and then relate then, comically, with several other images already existing in their mind. These comical connections utilize both sides of the brain; promote visualization, thereby resulting to better absorption, retention and recall of data.

If you want to memorize a bunch of playing cards, attach them mentally, one by one to objects like doors, windows, or to bedposts in your bedroom which is very familiar to you. When you make these mental attachments comical and exaggerated, recalling those playing cards, in order, will become easier.

Another proof of including humor to enhance learning was stated in 1994, by psychologist Stephen Schmidt, Ph.D., of Middle Tennessee State University, who made several Psychology undergraduates remember sentences like –

"There are three ways a man can part his hair parted, unparted and departed."

Instead of:

"Man can wear their hair with or without a part, unless they are bald",

The undergraduates were more successful in remembering the funny version rather than the plain one.

Advertising copywriters know this well and depend on the same principle to make their commercials memorable. They use short, catchy, visual and funny words or images to cause a knee-jerk in our brains, thereby creating a better recall.

Several years ago, a glue company showed dozens of people piled up and riding on an elephant. There were so many pled up that the elephant, though moving, was barely visible. Amusing? Yes, and it churned up the sales of that glue brand.

We, too, in our personal lives, remember and recollect funny happenings much more vividly than the plain and humdrum moments of our lives.

Thick Walls

A drunken Rexy, one late night, invites a drunken Dennis over to his apartment where there was very big brass gong hanging.

"What's the bell for Rexy?" asks Dennis.

"It's not a bell. It's a gong that nags," Rexy replied.

"A gong that nags? Oh, c'mon!

"Watch this," says Rexy. He grabs the dong and gives the gong an ear-shattering bang and waits. Seconds later, a shrill voice from the other side of the wall screams:

"Are you bloody out of your mind, you jerk! It's bloody 3:00 in the morning!"

A Sermon

In the wee hours of the morning, a drunk was in no shape to drive, so he wisely parked his car and walked homewards. As he was walking along unsteadily, he was stopped by a policeman.

"Where are you going to at such an hour?" asked the officer.
"I'm going to attend a sermon."
"And who is going to conduct this sermon, at this hour?" the cop asked.
"My wife, of course!"

"Humor is something that strives between a person's aspirations and his limitations. There is more logic in humor than in anything else. Because, you see, humor is truth."
Victor Borge

Chapter 6
Social and Economical

In my profession of corporate training, humor plays a key role in ensuring acceptance, lively interaction and an effective transfer of knowledge and skills. Humor, in the form of funny self-introductions, ice-breakers and other games quickly warms up and builds camaraderie amongst participants. A happy and an interactive class, usually, is open to new ideas and learns quickly. In a fun-filled atmosphere, even direct, assertive statements are accepted and absorbed with very little resistance.

The results are more than convincing, people like fun and amusement; and these generate positive feelings and compassion. With humor we understand ourselves better and also deal with others in a creative and a constructive way.

Positive, good-natured, kindly contemplations of the incongruities of life are beneficial in the work place and at home. Your sense of humor tells others that you are easy to work with, approachable and open to all kinds of feedback. Colleagues with a fine sense of humor help keep the atmosphere light and in check even during high stress situations.

Humor, in business transactions and interactions, makes you likeable, and when you are liked, you can assuredly gain the trust of others. Trust, as we all know, in business is crucial. Several years ago, I closed my biggest sale and maintained a long and easy relationship with a major client in New York because I used humor in my first interaction with them. For the rest of our, long-lasting, relationship business exchanges flourished because openness and trust had been perceived as part of my personality at the get-go level.

The parallels between good humor skills and great selling techniques are quite powerful. To create humor in a situation, the humorist learns to relate to his audience, riffs about what he saw and knows, lets his audience have it. The laughter generates excitement and energy in the audience. The humorist lets the energy rule. He leans back and pretends to let the audience take over and he lets them feel that it wasn't he who made them laugh but they laughed of their own accord.

Similarly, a salesperson generates rapport with his clients, asks questions to highlight needs, presents his product or solution, and leans back a bit for the energy and desire. The energy created in this manner makes the customer that they are buying the solution rather than feeling like someone is selling it to them. Thus, a professional salesperson closes many a deal with a subtle touch. Both skill-sets require confidence in self, in product and an ability to connect, engage and then influence. That's why people with a large funny bone also bring home a large paycheck.

Humor at work is also a great team-building tool. People who have shared fun and laughter together share a special bond and light- heartedness about their relationship. Daniel Goleman, the author of "Emotional Intelligence and Primal Leadership", refers to laughter as that act which nurtures the open loop nature of man. Meaning, just as we need air to circulate through our lungs, water through our kidneys and nourishment through our body, we also need thoughts and emotions to run smoothly through our hearts, minds and in exchange with others. We need to have a consistent give and take of emotions with others to survive. Laughter, claims Daniel Goleman, catalyzes our open-looped, emotional exchanges fast-tracks trust and empathy between us and others.

My parental home back in India was constantly filled with laughter. My siblings, cousins and I would often get together and spend hours and days cracking up one another with jokes, gags, mimicry and skits. The fun was always harmless and laden with love for each other. Till today, my family members cherish the memories of those fun-filled days of laughter at home.

Currently, at home with my kids in the Philippines, this culture of cracking up has been inherited and still thrives. My home is filled with heaps of books and quality literature that can all be classified under humor. The movies and the shows we generally prefer are almost always labeled "comedy". My kids have developed a keen sense of humor and are gentle, quick-witted and fun. Time spent at home is usually time surrounded by gay laughter. It is my belief that the gift of laughter has made my children compassionate, forgiving and open-minded to all creeds and cultures. At the core of all humor at home, we have discovered humility and a lust for joyful and wholesome living. Though, there are times that I have sneaking suspicion that it is money that keeps my kids close to me but in my heart I know it is the humor that binds us. It is true that a family that laughs together stays together.

The visible and the hidden effects of humor are also good for business and the economy too. Happy workers and executives are productive workers. Teams that trust each other produce optimum results. Effective teams and communities help develop organizations and build nations at a fun-filled, lightning pace.

I am sure, by now, you are convinced enough to pick up a joke book and memorize it from end to end. I assure you that with the techniques you will learn here, in this book, buying a joke book will really not be necessary. Gracias!

Too Early!

Three men line up at the Pearly Gates, and the Angel asks them, "All three of you are very early what happened?"

First Man: Sir, I was very late for work and as I ran out to catch a bus, while trying to put on my shirt a refrigerator fell on my head and killed me instantly.

Angel: That is weird! Stand aside..................... What's your reason?

Second Man: I'd forgotten my wallet at home. When I got to my bedroom, my wife was hurriedly fixing herself and I smelled cigar smoke. When I looked out the window, I saw this man running so I picked up our refrigerator and threw it at him. The exertion gave me a heart attack and I died.

Angel: This is getting really strange! Stand aside, please........... And, Sir, what brings you here so early.

Third Man: Sir, I don't know what happened, I was quietly sitting inside a refrigerator and having a smoke when I died.

Section 3

CREATING HUMOR

"The whole object of comedy is to be yourself and the closer you get to that, the funnier you will be."
Jerry Seinfeld

Chapter 7

Humor Belief System

Is a sense of humor natural a genetic trait? Well, let me see! How many cavemen did it take to light a fire? The answer: None, because there was no such thing as a fire then.

Humor like any other trait is fifty percent natural, fifty percent nurture and a hundred percent warped point of view.

A couple of years ago at a meeting of local training professionals, one of us, a foreigner amongst us, made a massive "faux pas". He expressed the belief that trainers and speakers from the west or overseas were better and more able than the ones from Asia.

In the room were a little over a dozen of us. There were a few ladies, more men and almost all of us Asian, except for two. Everyone was aghast and insulted at his bigoted outlook and we didn't know what to say or do. Stay and suffer the indignity, or, stand up and just walk away? We were all educators of sorts, trained to be appreciative, assertive and forward-looking. The perpetrator turned red in the face and was trapped in a tense and disastrous situation of his own making.

Over the preceding months, we'd been meeting with him and talking about setting up a professional consultancy group. We'd covered issues pertaining to costs, time systems, opportunities, cultural diversity, core values and purposes. We'd also tackled an educated and business person's code of ethics for a team made up of different experiences and ethnicities.

At that time, I was a new student of Appreciative Inquiry* [1] and also Humor. I was completely Asian yet cosmopolitan in experience and outlook. Something inside me was telling me that the leadership of the group, at that moment, was my calling. I couldn't defend his error and I couldn't ask everyone else to let it just pass. The work and time we had put into the business at hand and our abilities to overcome such disasters were at stake. I was also sure that everyone else was entertaining similar thoughts but didn't know what to do. The room began to stink of a death–like silence. Time, seemingly, had stopped. I had to do something!

With extreme caution, making no eye contact with others, without any highs or lows in my voice: I began to speak slowly.

"So this guy walks into a bar …etc., etc." No one reacted. I went on with another, *"Back in the medieval times, they had this archery contest…etc., etc.,"* No movement yet, but, with caution, I added a little drama and inflection to my voice and went on, *"So this socialite was playing cards when her butler called up…etc., etc."*

The jokes had no relevance and context to the moment and the meeting, but soon someone breathed. Another

---

[1] [*Appreciative Inquiry is based on a reverence for life and is essentially bio-centric in character. It is an inquiry process that tries to apprehend the factors that give life to a living system and seeks to articulate those possibilities that can lead to a better future. **Dr. David L. Cooperrider in Positive Image, Positive Action**]

one moved. Another one cleared his throat. One colleague looked at me and made a face. Slowly, the whole group began to breathe, move, made eye contact, and heaved a sigh of relief and the world slowly nudged forward.

At the end of what seemed like eternity, people began to talk and, unanimously, agreed to put off all further discussions till another time. Though the tension had been diffused at that moment, the wounds left were deep and had to be nursed at a time and a place away from that meeting room.

The group had gelled a bit because of the time and efforts invested together but, because of that "faux pas" it never became a team. Those from the group that still meet, never talk about the incident. But the scars of those wounds can still be felt and seen through their avoidance of talking about that incident.

Corny, irrelevant humor, on that day, did not save a business but did help overcome a crisis and prevent possible strangling of a bungling foreigner.

As you grow into this business of humor and get to master its skills and techniques, humor will prove itself as a revelation and a balm. Your belief in humor will deepen for its healing powers and capacity to convert catastrophes into things manageable and humane. A quick sense of humor, often, will become your redeeming grace.

Use humor often. Use it with sensitivity and discretion. Use it to help, encourage and exalt others. A deep trust in the powers and the benefits of humor will lighten your soul and strengthen your gratitude for the gift of life.

Here is a four-step approach to letting humor become a part of your personality and belief system:

Be: For having a lot more than just a bit of wit you've got to *be.* Just *be.* You've got to be present in the moment and active mentally and emotionally. And, you've got to become a part of the environment that surrounds you. You need to be immersed into what is happening around you.

Observe: To discover and capture the lopsidedness of life you need to become highly observant of all that is happening. You've got to listen well and you need to learn to observe yourself in the environment and the action from an outsider's perspective. Watch over yourself as an angel would and see yourself funny, failing and falling victim to life's shenanigans.

Respond: In the process of creativity there are no good or bad ideas. They are ideas and imaginations that are sometimes wild and berserk. What counts for humor is the active and instantaneous application of these ideas. Analysis will create paralysis. Take action; respond quickly and with wit even at the *risk* of failing or looking foolish. That is fun!

Emote: As and when your deliver thought actively, make effort to emote, characterize, dramatize and become the part. At this instant surrender your angelic perch and become a mortal in the midst of mayhem and mirth.

Employ these principles often and with speed. Soon you will become a wit who will never be a **BORE** in any circumstances.

Now I guess you may have had just about enough of talking about Humor. It is time to start creating humor on call. Let's get on with the first technique.

Technique #1

Now here is what I want you to do. I want you to go to the mirror and size yourself up. Look, in your appearance, for at least two things that are highlights of your looks. Look for things about yourself that are good looking and things that others would notice at first glance.

In my case, it is my eyes. When strangers look at me they get transfixed. Followed by my eyes people usually compliment me on the shape of my nose. This is more so in the Philippines where I live, and where noses are not as angular as mine. You do not have to believe me if you do not want to, all I am trying to do is make a point.

So back to you in the mirror! Look for something that really stands out:

List down these two or more physical attributes [easily seen/known to others] of your own that you are extremely proud about:

For example: luscious hair, lovely eyes, towering height, nose, lips, dimples, chest, breasts, and narrow waistline, pronounced derrière, anything!

Create a sentence using an adjective to describe your attractive feature and add "I love".

Step 1:

"I love my tantalizing eyes"

Now think of the most radical yet positive reaction it brings about in other people when they notice your attractive feature. For example: Do they gasp? Do they stare? Do they faint?

Next, expand: rewrite your sentence adding the reaction:

"I love my tantalizing eyes because they make ladies want to take me home."

Now, this sentence is slightly amusing but not yet funny. Exaggerate a little more and rewrite.

Step 2:

*"I **love** my tantalizing eyes because they make rich, old ladies want to take me home."*

Now this went from slightly amusing to amusing. Remember humor is about shock, surprise and derailment of logical thinking patterns.
By changing the word "love" into "hate" rewrite the sentence as follows;
Step 3:

*"I **hate** my tantalizing eyes"...long pause, look around, wait for frowns and then add..." because they make rich, old ladies want to take me home."*

What we have done is downplayed an attractive feature of your appearance and contrasted it with an exaggerated funny reaction. When you say, *"I **hate** my tantalizing eyes"* people in their minds go, "why?" and they start to rationalize and are tempted to want to convince you otherwise.

That is when you give them the contrasting reaction and flip their minds. This is incongruence, in action, created twice and created fast. And, the result? Suspense, surprise and laughter!

Creating laughter will take effort and time. Hold your breath and travel with me patiently all the way.

Let's call this technique as ***Hate Your Highs*** *and try another example.*

Step 1: *"I love my aquiline nose."*

Step 2*: "I love my aquiline nose because it makes people want to hang pictures from it."*

Or,

"I love my long, aquiline nose because it makes people want to hang their umbrellas from it."

.Step 3*:*

*"I **hate** my long, aquiline nose" ...long pause, look around, wait for frowns and then add… "because it makes people want to hang their umbrellas from it".*

So, go ahead and work upon your good looks, **Hate Your Highs** and make others laugh.

Technique #2

One more time go stand in front of the mirror and give yourself another once over. Yes, I do mean you! Remember the mind is not separated from the body. Just thinking about something will not get us there. We've got to take action. Please, to the mirror, now!

In front of the mirror size yourself up and look for physical attributes that you would willingly do away with. No, change that. Look for physical attributes that you do not like. No, change that again! Look for physical attributes that make you feel like burying your head in the sand and bidding the world goodbye!

In my case it is my teeth. My teeth remind me of a close-up of Tyrannosaurus Rex from the movie, Jurassic Park. Besides my teeth, I am also conscious of my fine, oily and mouse-colored hair. I am also conscious of my very bushy eyebrows that are now turning grey. My eyebrows remind of the big, hairy, bad guys from old, Charlie Chaplin movies. You do not have to believe me if you do not want to, all I am trying to do is make a point.

So back to you in the mirror! Look for something that really stands out:

List down two or more physical attributes [easily seen/known to others] of your own that makes you feel like committing *hara kiri.*
For Example; a balding head, a pronounced chin, frog-eyes, large ears, oversized belly, undersized chest - anything!

Create a sentence using an adjective to describe your unattractive feature and add "I hate"

Step 1:

"I hate my large ears"

Now, chances are that you could become touchy and sensitive at this stage. And, that actually is a good sign; do remember that no person with his head full of hot air can make others laugh. Others will snicker at him, behind his back, but he cannot make them laugh.

So come on down from your high horse and find fault in yourself. If you are unable to do so then have your significant [insignificant] other and look for faults in you. This will also let them have a good time [if not a heart-attack] at your expense. [Chances are while doing this you may attain humor enlightenment and write a book on humor yourself.] Go let your spouse or sweetheart nit-pick for you and at you!

Humor and laughter between members of the opposite sex creates an increased flow of oxytocin, an internal aphrodisiac or that magical group of fluid cells which make two people see floating hearts around each other's heads while at a bar, at the office water-cooler and sometimes even in a house of prayer. Letting your significant other nit-pick upon you may have exciting fringe benefits. Trust me! [Wink! Wink!]

Back to your unattractive feature! Think of the most radical and negative reaction it brings about in other people when they notice it. For example: Do they gasp? Do they stare? Or, do they faint?

Step 2:

Expand and re write your sentence adding the reaction:

"I hate my Mickey Mouse-like ears because they eavesdrop upon others even when I don't want to."

Funny? Just a bit. Let's try again.

"I hate my Mickey Mouse-like ears because"...pause...look around...go deadpan and add, "they eavesdrop upon my husband's fantasies even when I don't want to."

Now create the incongruence between what appears and what you say. Change "I hate" to "I love", re-write and add a Texan accent.

Step 3:

"Ah jus' love my Mickey Mouse-like ears because"...pause...look around...go dead-pan and add, *"they eavesdrop upon my husband's fantasies even when Ah don't want to."*

Much better? Maybe. Let's call this technique as ***Love Your Lows*** and work on another example.

Step 1: "*I hate my colossal backside."*

Step 2: *"I hate my colossal backside because people make way whenever I head for the buffet table."*

Or,

*"I hate my colossal backside because people make way, **very quickly**, whenever I head for the buffet table."*

Or,

*"I **love** my colossal backside because people make way, **very quickly**, whenever I head for the buffet table."*
***Step 3**:*

*"Ah jus' **love** my colossal backside" ...pause...look around...and add "because people **scramble for cover**, whenever Ah' head for the buffet table."*

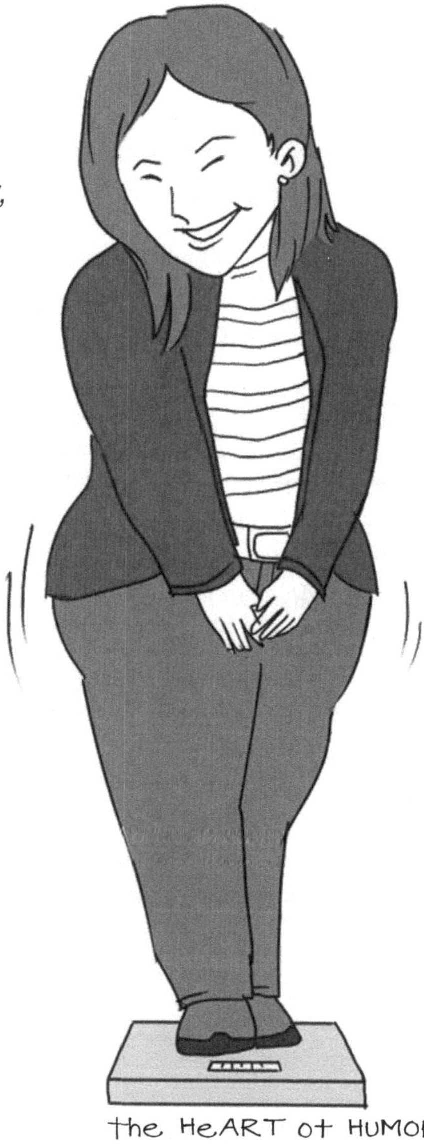

Again, as in Hate Your Highs, you have first created a suspenseful set-up that is in contrast to what appears and then you have tripped your listener's minds by saying something totally unexpected and outrageous.

Now at this stage, I am sure that you have noticed that in both techniques the perpetrator and the victim of the joke have been you.

This is a crucial learning in mastering humor - laugh and the world will laugh with you. Laugh at yourself and the world will have a party.

So, go ahead and work upon your good looks, **Love Your Lows** and make others laugh.

"Humor is an affirmation of dignity, a declaration of man's superiority to all that befalls him."
Romain Gary

Chapter 8
Attitudinal Development

Psychoanalyst Sigmund Freud has a take on humor which leads us right into assessing the attitude needed to be funny. Freud believed, as we grow and mature, the dreary grind of life and the entrapments of rationalizing all that exists, makes us slowly cheat ourselves out of the child within us. Thus, our desire for humor and laughter and our lust for life are constant and desperate attempts to regain and reclaim the lost pleasures of childhood. As children, no effort was needed to bring laughter into our lives. We had no need for canned jokes, stand-up comedy or anything else. We laughed at everything and we played for sheer pleasure. Fun, enjoyment and laughter were natural and the normal perks of the sunny mornings of our lives.

To be funny, essentially, requires that we loosen our girdles; de-starch our collars; let loose our hair; twirl our mustaches and, get down from those high horses of position and authority that we mount and ride upon, at the start of every single day. It is possible for each one of us to be funny, and we must also develop a deep, burning desire and intention to be funny.

You've heard of the saying that you can take a horse to the water but you cannot make him drink. To develop humor, just like any talent or profession, you must really, truly and sincerely want to succeed in it. You must want to make others happy. But hey, you have bought this book and read it this far! That is proof enough that you do have an intense craving for highlighting the ridiculous in life in kindly and an artistic way. Please take a moment to pat yourself on the back or go back to the mirror and say, "You are OK, Dude!" [No? Dudette? Okay!]

Having the intention to be humorous is the first step which needs to be followed by learning and mastering the techniques to be funny. Your intention is the thought, and practicing the different techniques will be the action that will help you be a funnier you. Our personalities and all we are is part nature and part nurture. Every artistic expression, every creative output and every talent needs development and, it needs practice. Methods and disciplines have to be followed to convert a technique into habit into character and into personality.

Actor Robin Williams in his early days would barhop in search of work. While performing, Robin used to appear completely natural and extemporaneous, but backstage before the show, he'd tell his director or manager all the steps he was planning to do. All his apparent talent, besides being natural to him, was also in fact method, practice, and determination!

In one of my creativity workshops, a participant shared a story about this monk who entered a monastery with a desire to achieve higher consciousness and enlightenment. Being a modern day, well-educated person, he saw no relation between higher consciousness and the wearing of an orange garbs and shaving his head. Thus, he chose not to follow the seemingly superficial methods towards attaining elevated consciousness.

Years went by without him wearing the orange garb, though he meticulously studied and practiced through the books, lectures and the activities. Decades later, aged and still restless, he found himself nowhere near higher consciousness or enlightenment. Finally, nearing the prime of his life, out of sheer frustration, he had his head shaved and put on the orange garb of a monk. Kaboom! He was hit by a stroke of brilliant light. His body glowed, his spirits soared and every cell in his being was filled up with wisdom and profound spirituality. He attained the kind of spiritual awareness and enlightenment he had been desirous of all his life. The heavens for him, seemingly, opened up and he felt as if he was reborn. Suddenly, in the next instant, again, Kaboom! He collapsed, and died on the spot.

Mastering creativity and humor is just like that–you will never know when the brilliant light will shine upon you. And daze and dazzle you it will as you move onwards and consume the theories, the beliefs, the attitude and the techniques methodically. The relationship between nature and nurture, between intent and method is just like the relationship between the chicken and the egg—you will never know which one comes first. Just remember, depending on your needs, to shave or duck before you hear the sound of Kaboom!

In all the techniques and skills you will absorb and learn a great fraction of your time will be spent getting into the fun mood. When exaggerating, you may want to pretend to be in a contrasting, somber and a depressive mood. When expressing something disappointing or sad, you might want to pretend to look happy and elated. When expressing fears and doubts, as a set-up, you might consider acting proud and pretentious. Building this mood that is incongruent with the words you utter leans back on Stephen Leacock's original theory on humor.

Comedian Jaspal Bhatti of India always appears pitiful and surprised through all his political chicanery. Rex Navarete, a comedian from the Philippines, recreates the mood and the attitude of a domestic helper, a young boy or an old man whenever he mimics them.

In essence a lot of humor will require us to draw upon the hidden actor in all of us. In the succeeding chapters, while tackling techniques, this visual-verbal incongruence will be highlighted and exemplified.

Technique #3

Every one of us has some kind of a negative quirk. Something that we think is part of our nature and something that, we suspect, others know about us. I was in the past, I believe, slightly obsessive compulsive. I used to like to see things in order, clean and well arranged. Though I would, many times, work on a cluttered desk, I'd get really restless and antsy. You have probably seen a sign that says, *"A clean desk is the sign of a sick mind."* Every time, I used to clean or arrange my workplace *that sign* scrolled through my mind like clouds in the sky.

Recently, I came upon another sign that neutralized the effects of the first sign. This one said, *"A clean desk is the sign of a much cluttered drawer."*

Nowadays, these two signs put together keep me happy and balanced. I don't feel as obsessed to clean or not to clean my desk or drawer. Whether they are cluttered or uncluttered, I still go about my day sane and smiling.

For this technique, what I'd like you to do is list a personality quirk which you consider negative. Remember to list a behavior and not a physical feature or an incident about you.

For example: Fickle-minded, finicky, claustrophobic, procrastinator, short-tempered, introvert, schizophrenic, etc....

The more negative the behavior the better it is for creating humor.

Write it down as follows:

Step 1:

"I worry about being obsessive compulsive"

Now think of the most radical consequences any one of this trait generates.

Do you spend a lot of energy, time or money because of it?

Do others gain or suffer from this behavior?

If you secretly like being obsessive compulsive what are the negative consequences of a trait opposite to being obsessive compulsive?
Being a litterbug? Being a bum? Being a parasite?

Let's take our negative trait a bit further.

Step 2:

*"I **worry** about being obsessive compulsive because I am constantly fixing other peoples' neckties and makeup."*
Now, change that.

Step 3:

*"I am **proud** of being obsessive compulsive"*...pause...go deadpan...let lines appear on your listeners' faces...*"because when, people walk away from me their hair and neckties are better arranged than before."*

That got a little better. Or, did it?

You decide.

And, always remember that what is funny to you may not be funny to others. In case of fun, like in most case, the customer is of prime importance.

The fun you create must be drawn from within you, your wit, but it must be focused out to your audience.

Let's call this technique as ***Whack Your Worries*** and do another example.

Step 1:

*I **worry** about being a procrastinator.*

Step 2:

*I **worry** about being a procrastinator because deadlines might go whizzing past me.*

Step 3:

*I am **proud** about being a procrastinator. It gives me a chance to become a collector of some classic, unfinished deadlines.*

Let's try one more example:
Step 1:

*I **worry** about being a* schizophrenic

Step 2:

*I **worry** about being a* schizophrenic *because we never are alone.*

Step 3:

I am ***proud*** *about being a* schizophrenic. *It definitely beats being alone.*

There you go, I hope you are beginning to enjoy this. Please go ahead, make my day, and get crazy with ***Whack Your Worries!***

Technique #4

Contrary to our negative quirks there are certain attributes about ourselves that we like and are openly proud of. Those that surround us know about these behaviors of ours and sometimes teasingly refer to them as our weaknesses.

I am constantly teased about my kindness and my habit of letting things go. Friends, sometimes, blame me for being too nice and too easily forgiving. Though I realize and sometimes fear that these traits of mine let others take undue advantage of me, I cannot help but continue with them because they support my value system and make me who I am.

For example when someone seeks help from, I usually give it promptly and without heed. Or, when someone needs to borrow money, I can cut back on my own spending and my lifestyle to support others. You may consider this noble but it is also, many a times, downright foolish.

Likewise, I am sure, you too may have some positive traits that you suspect my someday be your Waterloo. What I'd like you to do is list these positive traits and be candid without stroking your own ego. Take into consideration what others sense and have said about you.

List things like: Sucker for love, romantic, generous, tender, inquisitive, supportive, gregarious, outgoing, outspoken etc.

Now take a trait and form a sentence as follows:

Step 1:

*"I am **proud** of being romantic."*

Now think of the most radical and outrageous consequences such a trait generates.

Is your living room stacked to the rafters with love songs from the last two centuries?

Do others gain or suffer from this behavior?

Do you constantly fall in and out of love with the lost and the lonely?

Let's take this a step further and rewrite it as follows:

Step 2:

*"I am **proud** for being an old-fashioned romantic because I constantly end up dating grandfathers."*

Now, change that.

Step 3:

*"I **worry** about being an old-fashioned romantic"...*pause...go deadpan...let your listeners' brows furrow*...then add... " because I constantly end up dating grandfathers."*

Now that's a wee bit funny but for sure it's going to have the "Ye Ol Grandpa's Fraternity" chase me with their antique, newly 'Made in China' umbrellas.

Let's call this technique as ***Tarnish Your Traits*** *and take another example:*

Step 1:

*I am **proud** about being honest.*

Step 2:

*I am **proud** about being sincerely honest even though, at times, it makes me lose money.*

Step 3:

*I constantly **worry** about being honest because it, usually, isn't ever lucrative.*

There you go! I hope you have a good time with **Tarnish Your Traits.**

"A comedian's job is to make people laugh. But a humorist makes them laugh and then think. Humor is a way of life, a pattern of behaving. It's the ability to bend without breaking."

M. Dale Baughman

Chapter 9

Resourcing and Repackaging

The very first resource that we know of, by now, is our life and ourselves. From the humorist's point of view, everything about us is funny. Our looks, our thoughts, our opinions, our jobs, positions, material holdings, relationships, families and even our belief systems are resources for fun. When a humorist gets hungry, then the world, starting from where he is, becomes his grazing ground. He can go about the world, nibble and chew at anything and everything his heart desires.

In Hindustani, there is a saying, "To the one who is hungry for grass, everything appears green." So, when you reclaim your intent to look at the ludicrous side of life, you will find fun and frolic in every nook and cranny of our existence. Just as when you buy and drive around a green car, you naturally tend to notice all the other green cars. Likewise, in humor, when you develop the eye and the ear for it, you will notice that there are plenty of fun things to pick upon around us.

To master humor skills, you will have first have to experience it a lot. You may have to amass a personal reservoir of things humorous. You will have to begin by watching comedy movies, plays, stories, etc. You will have to keep track of what people find funny. You will have to discover how skillful and outstanding humorists observe, employ and deliver humor. You will have to put together a cornucopia of your favorite jokes, gags, one-liners, exaggerations, put-offs, etc. Soon, through overexposure and osmosis, you will develop an ear and an eye for good humor.

Nearly seven years ago, when I'd just began to really appreciate how humor helps, I was at a dinner with some friends when one of them began to jovially pick at me. I was surprised that I found it easy to respond with wit at every crack he took at me. Soon we both realized that we were humor students, we turned that evening into a show of laughter and light fun.

Till date, whenever we meet, we reminisce that evening of our acquaintance and of our bouts with laughter. Much of the material that you will initially collect may seem to belong to someone else. True, but overtime you will learn to morph it in such a way that it will become your own and your personality will adapt to it. Collecting the material, having a scrapbook or a humor file will give you insights into the comical side of life as expressed by others. Knowing and comprehending how others perceive life and living will build your humor muscles and strengthen your funny bone.

Across the world, jokes, gags and plays imitate and improve upon one another. No, don't worry, it is not plagiarism it is creativity and innovation! Gathering, deforming, reshaping, morphing, coloring, stripping and repacking is how new things and ideas usually come about. Shakespeare's "A Comedy of Errors" has influenced hundreds of other plays in different cultures and during different periods of time. Polish humor is sometimes converted to Irish, Irish to Norwegian, Norwegian to French to Arabic to Indian to Malaysian to Bicolano etc.., etc. Remember, humor is all about life in all its different colors and flavors. Also remember that originality is the science of concealing your resources.

Duplicating one source is called plagiarism; tapping into hundreds of resources is called research.

Ok, let's take a break and do some exercises again. Mind and body are just the same. Let our actions lead our thinking. Let's work a wee bit more!

Technique #5

We do know that humor is created through incongruence and that it can be packaged and presented through three forms of media: Physical, Visual and Verbal. By using descriptive or perception-changing words these three forms can be mixed or matched to create incongruence and therefore laughter.

Here's an example by Ronald Reagan:

"Politics is supposed to be the second-oldest profession. I have come to realize that it bears a very close resemblance to the first."

Or, try this one.

"Once we had Clinton, Johnny Cash and Bob Hope. Now we have Bush, no Cash and no Hope"

For this technique, I'd like you think of something about yourself that is different or has changed over time.

"In my case, when I was the age of my kids, I used to believe that one day I will change the world, but nowadays I consider myself lucky if my kids let me change channels on television."

This is true, you don't have to believe me if you don't want to. There was a time when people would consider my every uttered word as a prophecy. Now even after having authored books, I still have to hard sell my ideas.

So here's how to do this.

Step 1:

Take an example, incident or an issue from your life. For example: You turned fifty, you are 30 pounds heavier, you earn twice as much, etc....

Write it down as follows:

Thirty pounds ago, I could touch my toes a hundred times in a minute

Step 2:

Think of a radical contrast:

Nowadays it takes me a hundred minutes to put my socks on.

Or,

Nowadays, I consider myself lucky if I get to see my toes...

Or,

Nowadays, I just name them from where I am...Big Joe, Curly, Larry, etc.

Step 3:

Combine the statements and deliver with style and rhythm

"Thirty pounds ago, I could touch my toes a hundred times in a minute"...pause...project..."and nowadays, I just name them from where I am...Big Joe, Curly, Larry, etc...."

Remember, humor does not come easy. It takes a hundred edits and several trials before it gets funny. Let's call this technique as ***Compare and Contrast*** and I recommend you create examples from what is true for you.

Technique #6

Now for this little technique, I will not have you run to the bathroom mirror and neither will I force you into some soul-searching.

I will, though, want you to look at who you in a very critical manner. I would like to you take a warped look at who you are, what you do and what your social standing or status is. I would like you to look for something about you that makes you different, unique or even weird.

Like in my case, when I first came to the Philippines from India, my Filipino friends would have a hard time with my name Raju, which is similar to the Tagalog Radio, in pronunciation. One day, a friend of mine called me up and wondered aloud as to why I had so many cousins in the local appliance stores. I didn't quite get it until he read out the names of my cousins—Radio, Television, Transistor, etc.

Twenty-five years later, when I get on the phone with strangers, I still have to spend time correcting their pronunciation of my name. Many a times, I feel like taking the phone line and strangling some of those who giggle in the background.

Anyway, humor aside, let's get a little serious. Oh, ok, I mean let's get funny.

The thing is that there is always something about us that differentiates us from the rest and the stranger this is the funnier it can help you become.

So for this technique, look into your life and personality for something that is unique. Are you a little, brown-skinned person married to a, pink-faced man barrel of beer from Ireland? Are you a very tiny, slim man with a turban married to what looks like the map of Tamilnadu?

Ouch? Sorry!

So, look yourself up, take a look at your life and get started as I do.

Step 1:
I am an Indian and my wife is a Filipina.

Do we eat Masala Dosa with Kare-Kare?
Do I wear a loin cloth while she a pair of denim jeans?
Do we have kids that pout their snouts for pointing and shake their heads for saying yes? I like that one!

Step 2:

I am an Indian and my wife is a Filipina and if ever our countries go to war, my kids will end up shaking their snouts and pointing with their heads.

Uh, not funny enough! Let's take another shot at it.

Step 3:

I am an Indian and my wife is a Filipina and if ever our countries go to war, my kids will end up being Mali-Asians who point with their snouts and agree with a head bob.

There is a little bit of local humor and context involved in this set-up and punch. The pun is in the word "Mali: which means "wrong" in Filipino and the compound sounds like "Malaysians."

Not too funny. A bit local but you do get the picture?

No? Okay, here are a few more examples:

My Mom's a Psychic and my Dad's a Historian. Between the two of them, I never know whether we are gone today or here tomorrow.

My Dad's an Analyst at the Institute of Economics…his job is to record practice and study if it will work in theory.

My Mom's a Lawyer, Dad a Doctor…between the two of them they got a great thing going…she robs people and he kills them.

Or, here's a stretched out, interactive one for the Indian in the Philippines:

How many Indians in the Philippines do you know with the name Raju?
Five, six.

What do you suppose is the average height of the Indian in the Philippines?

Five, six.

What is the most common business of the Indian in the Philippines?

Five, six.

This one is "ouch" all the way for the Indian in the Philippines. "Five, six" is the nick name hurled at many Indians who by profession are loan-sharks. They lend five and collect six.

The humor is very demeaning but, it beats being insulted about the smell of spice on our skins, the way our snouts are sliced and the surplus of hair on our bodies. Grrr!

You need grace and dexterity in choosing your pain and pleasure while using **Undo Your Uniqueness.**

Small Stuff

My Dad's a specialist. He knows an awful ***lot*** *about some awfully small stuff*

Timing Is Everything

Pido shows up late for work. His boss yells, "You should've been here at 9:30!"
Pido replies, "Why? What happened at 9:30?"

Knows Everything

In every organization, there will always be one person who knows what's going on. This person must be fired.

"Life does not cease to be funny when people die; just as it does not cease to be serious when people laugh."

George Bernard Shaw

Chapter 10
Sensitivity and Timing

At this stage, should you still be wondering if it is at all possible for you to be funny and creative? Let me tell you what I usually tell all my workshop participants:

If you are:

- *short or tall or just square*
- *fat or thin or just lumpy*
- *single or married or plain lost*
- *male or female or anyway fabulous*
- *rich or poor or still undecided*
- *slow or fast or plain out gas*
- *black or white or just a thriller'*

You can be funny! Yes!

No matter who, what you are or what you do for a living, you can be brilliant and funny in your very own way. You are unique, just like everyone else.

This almost always makes us potential candidates for someone else's ridicule. If it is possible for us to be a target, then our own wit also can be the key for *kindly contemplation and the artistic expression of our own follies and foibles.*

Surely you are thinking-"if I pick on something, someone or some incidents, will I be hurting others feelings?" The answer is yes. You will be making some one go "Ouch" most of the time.

The solution for this malady and the number one role to sensitivity in being funny is that first and foremost, you must pick upon yourself. Yes, you might as well pick upon yourself and laugh at yourself because, in many ways, there is always someone laughing at you. Beat them to it and laugh at yourself first and keep in mind that you can never sue your own self for slander. Amen!

Your humor must be self-effacing. Talk about your own size, shape and idiosyncrasies. Should you pick upon your own ethnicity, culture and belief system then make sure that you are on common ground with your audience. Try to pick upon issues that you all accept and agree upon. For example, Indians like to claim that you can take an Indian out of India, but you never can take India out of an Indian. This will go well if you are an Indian and are saying this, non-sarcastically, amongst a friendly group. This may not bear well if some non-Indian says this of Indians by way of criticism.

The Spaniards refer to this as "delicadeza" and they also like to refrain from discussion of politics and religion because people can be strongly opinionated about these topics. Similarly, be careful and cautious of picking upon people because of their color, caste or creed. You might ask if this is at all possible. As mentioned earlier, all humor does create an "Ouch" for someone or of a system. What you have to do is check the tone and the mood of a situation and deliver the "Ouch" in such a way that it tickles rather than scratches.

Make humor about nature, geography, the traffic, food, global business, trends, fashions and liberally pick on celebrities and icons because all these are fair game.

Convey your insights and observations in the least abrasive fashion while exaggerating in a polite and mild way.

Try these one-liners on for size and see how they fit into being sensitive with humor.

"Teach a child to be polite and courteous, and when he grows up, he'll never be able to edge his car onto the freeway!"

"If it is true that we are here to help others, then what exactly are the others here for?"
[At this the guy with a stiff mustache might respond, "Uh-duh, they are here to help you."]

You noticed that both one-lines here pick upon universal manners and values of common courtesy. Both of them are creative expressions of the realities of life. Therefore, make efforts at enlarging your funny bone but let it stay benign.

[By the way, I did pick upon men with stiff mustaches. Oops! Sorry! I will make sure to grow one by the time this book hits the stands. Write me to find out if I've kept my word.]

True-blooded humorists have great timing. Humor not delivered while the iron is not hot anymore generates no fun. You may have heard about the wit of Sir Winston Churchill and the exchange between him and a hoity-toity Lady Astor

Lady Astor to Sir Winston Churchill: "Winston, if you were my husband, I would flavor your coffee with poison."

Churchill to Lady Astor: "Madam, if I were your husband, I should drink it."

That retort of Churchill couldn't have created any impact had it been delivered a few pauses, moments later. It had to instantaneous.

Last year in Chicago, early in the day at a friend's place, one of his elderly lady friend and I were chatting about changing traditions and values in sex amongst teenagers. We spoke about how in our days, talk of sex and sex-related subjects were taboo. And, how many of us hadn't even heard of contraceptives when we were still young.

A while later, as all three of us were stepping out for a Sunday brunch, my friend Elmo did a final check of his apartment to see of he'd switched off the lights, locked the windows and turned off the cooking range, etc.... When done, he turned and asked us if we'd forgotten anything. His elderly lady friend made as if she was going to say something and then stopped. "What?" asked Elmo, looking a bit perplexed and anxious. She looked at him blankly, paused long and said in a deadpan fashion— "condoms?"

Both Elmo and I, with the discussion of the morning still fresh on our minds, burst-out laughing! Derailment was done and delivered with one single word and at the most lethal moment. In Stand-Up Comedians lingo, "She killed us bad!"

Comedians, actors, speaker and all artists know and respect the value of perfect timing. A moment that is not used well will never come back again no matter what. Likewise, humor delivered at a wrong time also can cause harm rather heal. With practice and patience, our intuitive skills get sharpened and we learn to be lethal with our timing of humor. Eventually, with heightened sensitivity and timing we become healers of souls through humor.

Several years ago, in our thirties, me and a bunch of my friends lost a dear friend possibly through murder. He had been killed, torched and left alongside a highway. All of us and his family were aghast at the incident. The pain was excruciating and for days and weeks we just couldn't put together a laughing, joyful image of a living him to that mass of scarred bones-and-flesh sight of him.

Every single moment, from the time he'd been found on the road till the time of his cremation, our moods fluctuated from deep anguish to shock to rage. Eventually, after his last rites, in the depth of our beings, we found a desire to go on living and slowly laugh.

To this day, I am sure, that when we finally began to relieve our spirits from the clutches of darkness, it was the proper time to do so. I remember, at the end of his funeral, I began to, quite unconsciously, hum a song that he used to so love. My friends soon followed suit and then sang along with me. Later on we relaxed and began to share pleasant and joy-filled stories about him. The timing of our release from the pain was just right because the excruciating pain, as per Mirza Abdullah Ghalib, slowly began to transcend us. The moment was naturally and gracefully decided upon in our hearts, at a time and place where grief and joy meet.

In everyday life, whenever we turn up our humor skills and attitudes, we do need to also turn up the sensitivity of our hearts toward the feelings, the state of mind of the people around us. Remember, humor is rooted in humility and kindness even though it yells out a proud "Yes!" to life. Yes!

And now for the last time, raise yourself and attend your inner calling to be funny. Let's do another exercise!

Technique #7

This one is also known as the good news, bad news technique. Here's a wonderful example:

Doctor to Patient: The bad news is that your feet stank and we had to cut them off… and the good news is that someone's made a wonderfully, great offer on your shoes.

For this technique write down a current incident, at home or at work, that may have disappointed or elated you.

For example: Wife elopes, company moves, you turn fifty, etc.

Step 1:

Make the negative statement, *"Wife elopes with the family driver."*

Now take the bad news and make it sound worse-

"Young wife runs away with nasty, old family driver"

Step 2:

Now take look at the bright side.

"You will have two less people to worry about"
Make it outlandish and give specifics.

"You will have two less gifts to prepare this Christmas."

Or

"You will now save on shopping expenses and a salary of one.

Step 3: Put the two statements together.

"The bad news is my young wife ran away with the nasty, old family driver." …pause…look worried and pitiful… and slowly and loudly add, "The good news is I will now have to buy two less gifts this Christmas."

This technique is slightly reversed in fashion compared to making straightforward speaking. It teaches you to think out of the box, get radical and use the flip side. It also lets you heal from life's little shenanigans much more quickly.

Let's call this technique as ***Neuter Your News*** and try another example:

Step 1:

Bad news is you find out your tour guide in the Himalayas does not speak any English.

Step 2:

Good news is that he will laugh at every joke you make and you'll never know when the avalanche will hit you.

One more example:

Step 1:

The good news is that, after a long vacation, my mother-in-law is finally going home.

Step 2:

The bad news is she'll be right back as soon as she sells her house in the country.

Of all the techniques, this is the easiest and the funniest. That's why I saved the best for the last. Shall we name it ***Neuter Your News*** and have a ball!

"Jesters do often prove prophets."
William Shakespeare

Chapter 11
Leading with Laughter

Our world starts and ends with us, therefore, leadership must necessarily begin with us. If we do not seek out the light from the darkness, create new horizons or tread paths yet un-trodden for ourselves then we will not know how to lead.

"*Gnothi se aitton*" or "*know thyself*" was generally attributed to Socrates. However according to Plutarch, the ancient historian, this was first inscribed on the Sun God Apollo's Oracle of Delphi temple in ancient Greece. Shakespeare in "*Hamlet*" says "*This above all: to thine own self be true; and it must follow, as the night the day, thou canst not then be false to any man*."

Being true to oneself, knowing the self above all is the cornerstone for building a life that is authentic and a character that is awash with leadership abilities. The key to knowing, understanding and being true to ourselves requires the shattering of all pretensions. The breaking down of pretensions, the deflating of an artificial ego requires a recognition and acceptance of the self as to who and what we really are. The key to self-acceptance and to self-love, however, is utter humility and the main ingredient of humility is that spice of life called humor.

It is said that the meek shall inherit the earth and by meek they don't mean small and scared but someone who is kind, forgiving and most of all humble. I respect this value a lot and one incident in my life has made it a permanent part of my life.

Fresh Air

It was 1969, I was in my shorts. Yes please, you may take a moment to visualize me in my shorts. Spider legs!

I used to study in a Zoroastrian school, in India, called the Sardar Dastur Hoshang Boy's High School. In those days, hardly twenty years after the British rule, it still carried the Khaki culture. Kids wore Khaki uniforms and several teachers would dress in starched suits with safari-type, hard hats to go. The school campus was the size of ten football fields, had wooden buildings like military barracks. In summer the winds blew strong and dusty while in winter the skies were misty till noon.

Several teachers were of the Zoroastrian faith, some Hindus and only one of them was a Christian. Mr. Arpootharaj was stout, dark-skinned with Dravidian features. He used to pat his curly, black hair down with pomade and his most outstanding feature was a smile that could be seen a mile away. He taught us Science, English and Mathematics. He was kind, funny and always forgiving. And because of his nature, he was always at the receiving end of jokes and pranks.

Being a Christian teacher who taught Science, he'd often be seen marching the corridors of the school with the Bible, Darwin's "The Origin of Species", a blackboard eraser and a box of chalks by his side. The moment he'd enter a class, he'd demand the windows be thrown open to let in fresh air. He used to pronounce fresh air with flair…fresh aaiyr! And, because of this the boys nicknamed him "Sir, Fresh Aaiyr!"

One summer day, Sir, Fresh Air, walked into class sans his brilliant smile but with a look that was distant and pensive. With the eraser, he wiped the big blackboard clean once, twice and until it was black, shiny. With his chalk, he then placed a dot, plumb in the center of the blackboard. Slowly, he turned to the class and stated that we'd be studying Astronomy today and eased himself silently in a chair and stared straight ahead, still pensive and distant.

The boys went wild. "What's that, Sir?", "Is that Astronomy, Sir?", "Is that fresh air, Sir?" He did not react nor respond. The boys continued heckling but he stayed silent and distant. The boys didn't know how to carry on. You cannot continue teasing a person who does not respond. The room turned silent and the silence grew such that a pin, if dropped, would be heard miles away.

After what seemed like a millennium, Sir Fresh Air stood up and began to speak.
"Imagine!" he said.
"Imagine that the blackboard and all the space beyond is the universe. Recognize that the universe has thousands of galaxies and that little dot in the center is the galaxy that we live in, our Milky Way."

"Imagine," he continued "that within that dot, which is our galaxy, lays our Solar System and within that Solar System is our Sun, the Planets with their moons and our Earth. Within our planet Earth is our country, our hometown and this school room with all of us inside it."
"All of that," he went on "is within the dot and more. Yet, we live a life that is filled with pride, distrust and hate."

With a long sigh and still pensive, Sir Fresh Air, slowly sat down. The silence in the room took over again. Outside the wind still howled and the dust still blew. The boys in the class didn't know what struck them. A while ago they were top of the heap and now they felt puny and negligible in their own minds. With a stroke of his chalk, the Bible-toting, funny little brown man with a dazzling smile had shattered our worlds and left us with a lesson in humility that would last us a lifetime.

The relationship between leadership, humility and humor can best be exemplified by this little anecdote: President Roosevelt and his friend, Naturalist William Beebe had this habit of, every once in a while walking out onto the lawn of the White House during late evenings, to look up into vastness of the star-filled night sky and then remind each other how little and petty they were in comparison to the universe. The thought humbled them, softened their egos, and let them laugh thus allowing them to attend to their positions of power with lightened and mellowed spirits.

Former U.S. President, Ronald Reagan, was well known for his histrionic sense of humor and humility. Even his most strident detractors would confess to being charmed by his joviality and natural warmth. His humor opened doors for him, allowed him to smash through blockades and personal challenges. Mr. Reagan's disarming attitude and style of communication earned him the moniker of "The Great Communicator".

A mastery over humor, allows building of good rapport and having good rapport is the cornerstone of a powerful communications style. A leader with a powerful style of communicating is charming, persuasive and most often than not, also effective. Leadership is about change and change can only be created if it is communicated well.

Many leaders, when they are riding ahead of the herd forget to turn around and check if the herd is still behind them. A good sense of humor is deeply soaked in humility and sensitivity and it creates within us a highly acute sense of self and other-awareness. It empowers us with a high sense of engagement and we, as leaders, simply do not surge ahead without making sure that others are following us. It is truly said that when you laugh the world laughs with you. Cry and the world laughs at you.

And many leaders, at the pinnacle of their careers, sometimes burn out and get tired from leading and motivating others. They start questioning the value behind all they do and deliver to the world. They are overcome with anguish about why the world is such a happy and sad place at the same time!

A Shiny Centavo

A few years ago, I too, was wondering where to get new strength and energy to keep on with the routine and rigmarole of life. I was wondering how to keep on leading, directing and inspiring my family, my friends, the communities I am part of and myself. Not being able to find answers, I went for a walk as I usually do whenever I need to do some thinking.

It was a sunny Sunday morning. At first, I was just struggling with my own troubles but soon the pleasantness of the day seeped into my being and I began to feel lighter and happier. After having walked a few blocks, I came upon a shiny centavo lying on the street. I picked it up out of sheer habit. My Grandfather, in the days gone by, used to say that every little centavo represents a drop of sweat, a grain of food or an ounce of hope for someone, somewhere. I do know and realize that a centavo doesn't go far these days. Times have changed, massively, but a centavo to me still means something as it also reminds of the happy and insightful times with Grandpa.

After walking around for a while longer, I came and sat down on the steps leading up to my home. My home has two gates and I stayed by the smaller walk-up gate. Though, I was feeling lighter and happier than a while ago, I still didn't have any ideas on how to find meaning and purpose in all the activities of my life. I still didn't know what I could tell or do to inspire my family, friends, community and most of all myself. Absentmindedly, I kept turning and flipping the centavo between my fingers. My eyes on the ground, the heaviness of spirit, of a while ago, was trying to creep back into my soul, when I saw a little red spot of light jump and dance on and around the steps where I was sitting. The little spot of red light seemed alive and like a little angel it snuck in and out of the crevices, the blades of grass and the pebbles on the ground. At times, it would slow down and then quickly jump and prance away.

Momentarily, I gasped in surprise thinking it was probably some kind of an insect that I hadn't seen before. A chuckle escaped my lips when I realized that it was just a reflection of the early morning sun on the red, copper centavo which I was turning and flipping between my fingers. I liked the show that was being put on for me. It unleashed the child inside of me and I gleefully began to turn and flip the coin faster and with more creativity. My own, private little show came alive and kept me amazed and entertained for what seemed like hours but were actually a few moments of child-like indulgence.

Eventually, I looked up and into the sun, my smile widened and I stood up feeling filled with life and renewed energy for the day. It dawned on me that life cannot be just one, happy continuous glow and each; every one of us doesn't have to be a hero, a leader all the time. Life, such as it is, is already wonderful and even though we must make efforts to continuously improve it, we must also learn to be content and enjoy the life we have.

All we have to do is be like the little shiny, dancing centavo between my fingers. All we have to do is keep staying active and involved even when, at times, we feel dumped by the roadside. All we have to do, whenever given a chance, is the best we can. We must flip and juggle the challenges and the successes that come our way and let the show of life go on. The energy and enthusiasm that we generally strive for need not necessarily just come from the depths of our soul; it can also just be a reflection of all that surrounds us. It can be the laughter and the love of family, friends and community. It can be the little, pleasant sounds of children playing in the sun. Or, it can be a reflection of that brilliant body of light and life-giving energy that holds the earth and all of us in its brilliant embrace every single day.

Surely, there will be moments when the sun does disappear behind dark clouds, but our deepest hearts know that it is up there somewhere, hanging in for us. During such times, when it does seem to be out of sight, it is time to rest, recuperate and gather up more spunk for tomorrow. It is time to let the pain slowly transcend into a cure and to go on with the show of reflecting, moving and dancing amongst the blades of grass and crevices of the road ahead. It is time to rediscover and nurture humor within the pain. Living a happy life is, as simple as that.

These and all other ideas listed form only a small part of the many benefits of indulging in humor and humor-related activities. I beseech you to take these ideas to heart, employ them with passion and slowly but steadily change the world into a happier place through laughter.

"Laugh and the world laughs with you. Cry and you simply get wet."
Cliff Thomas

the Heart of Humor illustrated . . .

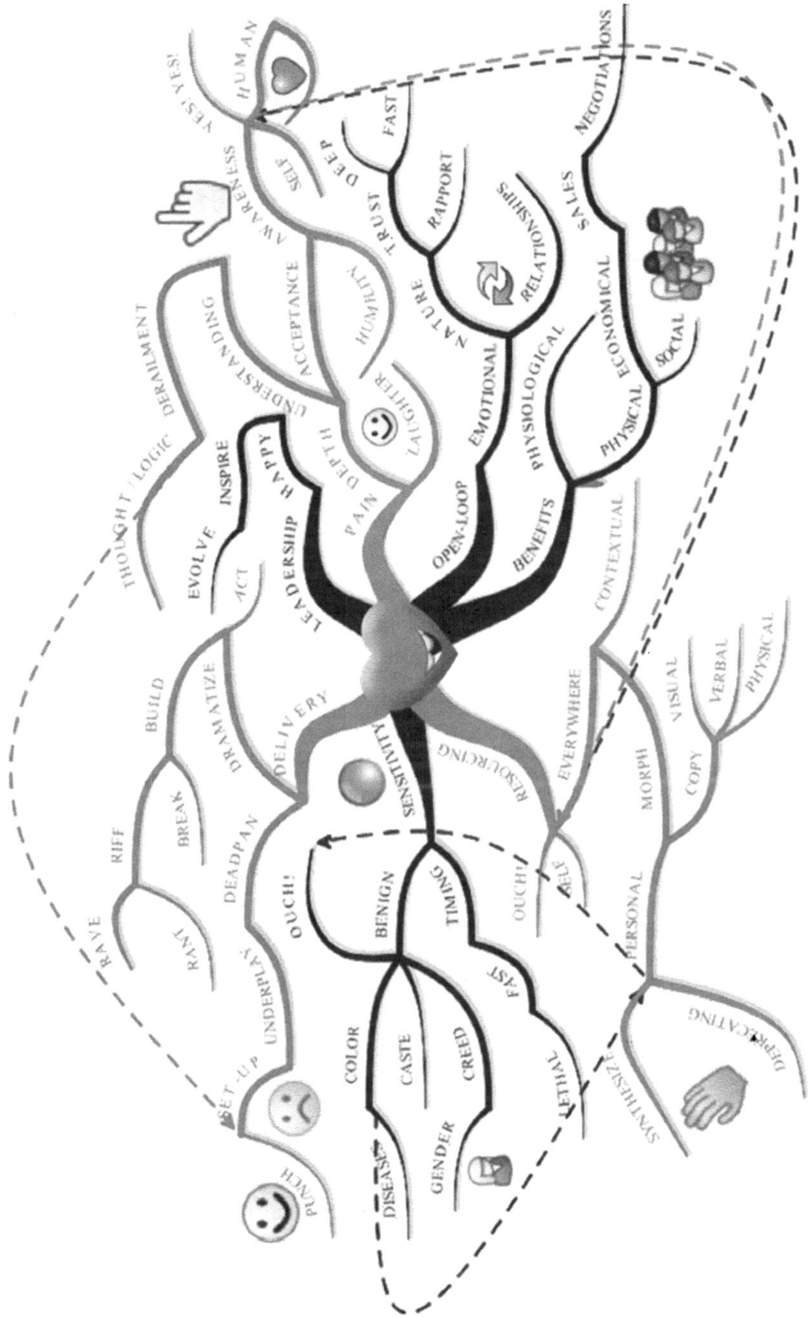

the Tales...

the Techniques...

about Inner Sun...

We at Inner Sun believe that every individual and every organization is a living system. At any given moment in this living system, there are three dimensions continuously at play.

The first is the dynamism that is innate, congenital, and embedded. In an individual, it is sometimes referred to as nature or personality; in a business organization, it may be referred to as "work culture".

The second dynamism is the one that exists outside of this system and is of many forms; the way that it is often referred to is the environment, economy, or ecology.

The third, the most vibrant, with a high potential to influence the inner and the outer dynamisms, is the dynamics of the process between the internal and external systems. The drivers of this intermediate dynamism are awareness, intelligence, emotion, memory, and action.

Inner Sun, the organization, focuses its own awareness, intelligence, and action towards this intermediary dynamism in all endeavors and interventions. The guiding elements behind our endeavors and interventions are:

Clarity of thought, words, and action;
Creativity of design, approach, and strategy; and,
Conscientiousness of purpose and ultimate objectives.

Thinking free of bias and mental hammerlocks leads to higher clarity, creativity, and conscientiousness. As individuals and organizations strive for that status, their intelligences expand, interests broaden, and achievements soar.

We provide:

- Business solutions and interventions that bring about measurable results;
- Trainers who judge success not on their own performances but by how much the delegates learn;
- Personal service and tons of great value in an atmosphere of inspiration, support, and motivation;

For details and a list of updated programs, please log on to *www.mandhyan.com*

about Raju Mandhyan

Author of five books, Cross-Cultural Leadership Coach and Learning Facilitator Raju Mandhyan has 15 years of experience in personal and organizational development. He has coached thousands of executives, delivered keynotes for hundreds of conferences across the Asian-Pacific region.

He is certified in Neuro Linguistic Programming, Mind Mapping, Appreciative Inquiry, American Management Association's Train the Trainer. He is also a Distinguished Toastmaster, Champion Speaker and the 2005-District Champion for Evaluations in the Philippines. In 2010, he had the rare honor of presenting at the American Society of Training and Development annual conference in Chicago.

Prior to his consulting career, Raju spent two years as an Engineer, two years as a Financial Consultant and 17 years as the CEO of an International Mercantile company handling projects for clients across the Mediterranean, Europe, Latin and North Americas. He has lived in India, USA and now lives with wife and three kids in the Philippines.

Look him up at www.mandhyan.com

other works

THE HEART OF PUBLIC SPEAKING

CREATIVE STARATEGIES AND TECHNIQUES FOR EFFECTIVE PUBLIC SPEAKING

Public Speaking is about ripping open your psyche and finding out what makes you worth anything, and it is about tearing down beliefs and then building new ones. This book provides you with creative strategies and techniques on how to choose the substance, build the structure and employ the style that'll help you effectively and delightfully add value to the lives of your audiences.

THE HEART OF STORY

CONNECT, ENGAGE AND INFLUENCE YOUR AUDIENCE CREATIVELY.

This is a fantastic job of bringing to our consciousness the what, why, and how of corporate storytelling. Stories are realities wrapped in roses, rainbows, and rhythm. This is, after all, what a company needs to sell, to build its brand, to communicate with stakeholders, and to drive creativity and innovation. THE HEART OF STORY is beautifully written and is such a smooth read.

THE HEART OF THE CLOSE

SUBTLE CLOSING STRATEGIES TO SOAR BEYOND YOUR SALES TARGETS

This book underscores a natural appreciation for the sales process. More than the "how-to's," real-life experience and wit weave throughout the book and how simplifies complex concepts. This amazingly insightful book comes at an opportune time, when the intricacies of selling in this milieu invite a more evolved appreciation for being human than a successful sales person.

what they say about the Heart of Humor...

Laughter is like magic - it comes and goes. Give it away as it comes; and the whole world will be laughingly with you - as this book has humanly outlined.

Rosalina O. Fuentes, Ph. D.,
The Laughing Dean, SAIDI School of OD

Humor is a reminder that no matter how high the throne one sits on, one sits on one's bottom ... never loose perceptive.

Donna Hickey MBA,
International Professional Speaker,
Chicago, Illinois.

Components of humor ripped apart so that even comedians can re-assemble their stuff funnier and faster.

Leo Martinez,
Actor and Comedian, Philippines

Practical tools and suggestions to dispense humor on demand.

Ajay Gupta,
Astrum Solutions, India

It's funny but humor really works and I should know! Learn, laugh and lead with "the Heart of Humor.

Scott Friedman,
Motivational Humorist.

Full of fun and foibles that make you ponder, explore and grow!

Janice Hung,
Model, Actress and Tai Chi Athlete

I've seen Raju make his audiences roll on the floor laughing. In this books he shows and tells how.

Bjorn Martinoff,
Fortune 100 Coach

Mandhyan has been able to take painful scenarios and play with them to create humor. And, he walks the talk!

Allie Mooney, APS,
Most Humorous and Entertaining Speaker, Year 2006,
National Speakers Association of New Zealand

Clear, sensitive and a delight! Through vivid stories and accessible strategies, Mandhyan wittily persuades how anyone can and should churn out humor for a more vibrant existence.

Sunita S. Mukhi,
Stony Brook University, New York

Up against the WALL? Read this book, it will open doors where none existed.

Mohan M Phadke,
Consultant, Pune, India.

Live Well, Love Much and Laugh often.